Services For
The Lenten Candles

Based On The Revised Common Lectionary
For Years A, B, C

Robert Jarbo

CSS Publishing Company, Inc., Lima, Ohio

*I dedicate this book to my two beautiful and
wonderful daughters — Elizabeth and Rebekah
— who never give me a dull moment.*

ISBN 0-7880-1553-2

Introduction

Symbols are so important in life because they draw us from the tangible, sometimes mundane world to a world of meaning where God is all the more realized to be present and active in all of life. In the same manner, candles are one of the most prominent symbols used today to remind one of the presence of God and the working of the Holy Spirit.

As candles are used during Advent for the Advent wreath, the Paschal candle during Eastertide, and the flaming candles during Pentecost, so too, candles can have an important role during the Lenten season. Just as the Lenten season reminds the Christian of Christ's journey to the cross, the seven candles and the weekly extinguishing of each one enhances that long, soon to be dark journey. When the last candle is extinguished and the darkness seems to be all-consuming, the darkness of the soul at the time of Christ's crucifixion is felt.

So is the intent of the services contained in this book. Although each Sunday during the Lenten season is considered a "little Easter" and is not really a part of the season, sometimes a small symbolic reminder is needed to cause us to think about where the season is headed — to the cross. Many Christians, as well as others in society, are not aware of the season of Lent with the same fervor as Advent and Eastertide. Symbolic reminders are needed to cause each one of us to reflect on our personal spiritual journey. Also, this collection provides an easy resource, based upon the lectionary, for services of extinguishing the Lenten candles. Pages with full instructions may be copied for the readers as well as the introits for the choir.

These services are flexible in that one or two liturgists may be used. Representatives from each Sunday school class can be used; I have used the confirmation class since they had been meeting at that time of the year. Examples are given as to how the services may be placed in the weekly bulletin.

The music is the same for each service though the lyrics are changed to fit the lectionary of the day. The harmonies are simple so that the introit would be appropriate for any size choir. If a choir is not available, then it is suitable for solo, two-part (SA), or trio (SAT). If a man and a woman are singing, it is suggested that the man sing the melody while the woman sing the alto.

The services are written for every Sunday during the Lenten season as well as Good Friday and Easter Sunday (when the Paschal candle is lit). If your church does not conduct a Good Friday service (since many churches in the community come together for that purpose), it is suggested to place it at the very end of the Passion/Palm Sunday service. The normal service would be at the beginning. As a result, on Passion/Palm Sunday, there would be two services of the Lenten candles so that all seven candles would be used.

The service for Easter Sunday (or Easter sunrise) does not extinguish a candle; rather, the Paschal candle is lighted. The choral selection is sung faster on this Sunday and has an extension on the end which gives it more of a joyous fanfare. If a soloist or duet is used on Easter, then the regular music is included with the Easter lyrics.

Now a couple of hints:

1. The candles. Buy purple candles. Purple is the proper color for Lent. After each service, pull out all the used candles and rearrange them so that the shortest candle is first, the next shortest, and so on. This way, one can save on buying extra candles and they will not look so uneven.

2. Do not place the seven candles on the altar table. If a floor candelabra is used, do not place it in the center chancel area. Remember, the Sunday services are considered "little Easters," so set the candles on a small table or place the candelabra at the side of the chancel area or on the lower level. It is not to be displayed prominently but in a place where it can be seen.

3. If you want to be creative, a "primitive" candelabra can be used. I suggest that the services of a carpenter in the congregation be used. In every church I have pastored, carpenters have felt honored when I asked them to build me an item. So make use of the talents in your church. Refer to the figure at the end of this introduction. It takes one 2"x4" piece of lumber cut into three pieces and assembled. My church had stored away two very old flag poles in iron stands, which we used as a stand for the candelabra. My volunteer carpenter cut the poles down to a proper height so that the candles can be reached, and a hole was drilled so that the candelabra

could fit snugly on the pole. I spray painted the wood a dark brown to match the pole. Make sure to give the carpenter a candle so that the proper size hole can be drilled. As a result, I have a simple, freestanding candelabra to use for Lent.

As you notice, in the service, a page for the readers is available with full instructions as to what to do as well as what to say. Just copy it, write their names on it, and give it to them. Nothing more needs to be explained. It is all contained on the page.

May this resource be helpful in your planning for this coming Lenten season.

Grace and peace to you from Jesus Christ.

Robert S. Jarboe

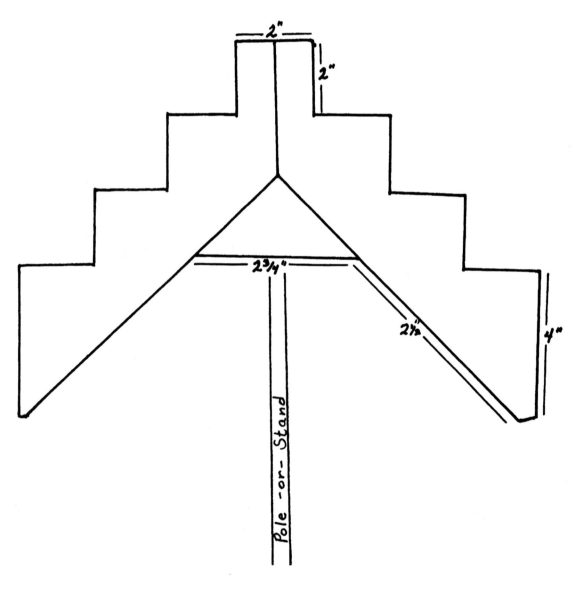

Revised Common Lectionary

(Used in the Lenten Candle Services)

Year A	Year B	Year C
First Sunday In Lent		
Genesis 2:15-17; 3:1-7	Genesis 9:8-17	Deuteronomy 26:1-11
Psalm 32	Psalm 25:1-10	Psalm 91:1-2, 9-16
Romans 5:12-19	1 Peter 3:18-22	Romans 10:8b-13
Matthew 4:1-11	Mark 1:9-15	Luke 4:1-13
Second Sunday In Lent		
Genesis 12:1-4a	Genesis 17:1-7, 15-16	Genesis 15:1-12, 17-18
Psalm 121	Psalm 22:23-31	Psalm 27
Romans 4:1-5, 13-17	Romans 4:13-25	Philippians 3:17—4:1
John 3:1-17	Mark 8:31-38	Luke 13:31-35
Third Sunday In Lent		
Exodus 17:1-7	Exodus 20:1-17	Isaiah 55:1-9
Psalm 95	Psalm 19	Psalm 63:1-8
Romans 5:1-11	1 Corinthians 1:18-25	1 Corinthians 10:1-13
John 4:5-42	John 2:13-22	Luke 13:1-9
Fourth Sunday In Lent		
1 Samuel 16:1-13	Numbers 21:4-9	Joshua 5:9-12
Psalm 23	Psalm 107:1-3, 17-22	Psalm 32
Ephesians 5:8-14	Ephesians 2:1-10	2 Corinthians 5:16-21
John 9:1-41	John 3:14-21	Luke 15:1-3, 11b-32
Fifth Sunday In Lent		
Ezekiel 37:1-4	Jeremiah 31:31-34	Isaiah 43:16-21
Psalm 130	Psalm 51:1-12	Psalm 126
Romans 8:6-11	Hebrews 5:5-10	Philippians 3:4b-14
John 11:1-45	John 12:20-33	John 12:1-8
Passion/Palm Sunday		
Liturgy of the Palms		
Matthew 21:1-11	Mark 11:1-11	Luke 19:28-40
Psalm 118:1-2, 19-29	Psalm 118:1-2, 19-29	Psalm 118:1-2, 19-29
Liturgy of the Passion		
Isaiah 50:4-9a	Isaiah 50:4-9a	Isaiah 50:4-9a
Psalm 31:9-16	Psalm 31:9-16	Psalm 31:9-16
Philippians 2:5-11	Philippians 2:5-11	Philippians 2:5-11
Matthew 26:14—27:66	Mark 14:1—15:47	Luke 22:14—23:56
or Matthew 27:11-54	or Mark 15:1-39 (40-47)	or Luke 23:1-49

Good Friday
(A, B, and C)
Isaiah 52:13—53:12
Psalm 22
Hebrews 10:16-25
John 18:1—19:42

Easter Sunday

Acts 10:34-43
Psalm 118:1-2, 14-24
Colossians 3:1-4
John 20:1-8
or Matthew 28:1-10

Acts 10:34-43
Psalm 118:1-2, 14-24
1 Corinthians 15:1-11
John 20:1-18
or Mark 16:1-8

Acts 10:34-43
Psalm 118:1-2, 14-24
1 Corinthians 15:19-26
John 20:1-18
or Luke 24:1-12

Bulletin Inserts For Year A

(R - Reader; P - People)

First Sunday In Lent

Service Of The Lenten Candles   Reader: _____
    Choral Introit
    Litany   From Psalm 32:19-22
    R: We have a wonderful God!
    P: Those of us who honor and trust him can see all the blessings he has for us.
    R: Praise God for his great kindness
    P: for he answers our cries for help.
    Scripture   Romans 5:12-19
    Extinguishing Of The First Lenten Candle
    Prayer
    Choral Introit

Second Sunday In Lent

Service Of The Lenten Candles   Reader: _____
    Choral Introit
    Litany   From Psalm 121:1, 2, 8
    R: Where do we find help?
    P: All help comes from our Creator God.
    R: How much will God protect us?
    P: God will protect us always and everywhere.
    Scripture   Romans 4:1-5, 13-17
    Extinguishing Of The Second Lenten Candle
    Prayer
    Choral Introit

Third Sunday In Lent

Service Of The Lenten Candles   Reader: _____
    Choral Introit
    Litany   From Psalm 95:2, 3, 7
    R: With thankful hearts, let us worship God.
    P: He is the greatest over all.
    R: We are the people of God.
    P: So we need to listen to him.
    Scripture   Romans 5:1-11
    Extinguishing Of The Third Lenten Candle
    Prayer
    Choral Introit

Fourth Sunday In Lent

Service Of The Lenten Candles   Reader: _____
    Choral Introit
    Litany   From Psalm 23:1, 6
    R: God cares for us like a loving shepherd.
    P: We find rest and refreshment.
    R: God's love and kindness is always with us.
    P: And we will live forever.
    Scripture   Ephesians 5:8-14
    Extinguishing Of The Fourth Lenten Candle
    Prayer
    Choral Introit

Fifth Sunday In Lent

Service Of The Lenten Candles   Reader: _____
    Choral Introit
    Litany   From Psalm 130:4, 5, 7, 8
    R: We worship a forgiving God.
    P: And we wait and trust on his promises.
    R: Only God has the power to save — so trust him.
    P: We are saved from our wrongdoings.
    Scripture   Romans 8:6-11
    Extinguishing Of The Fifth Lenten Candle
    Prayer
    Choral Introit

Passion/Palm Sunday

Service Of The Lenten Candles   Reader: _____
    Choral Introit
    Litany   From Psalm 118:19, 20, 27
    R: Let us enter God's gates of justice with thankful hearts.
    P: Anyone who is right with God can enter.
    R: This is God's day to celebrate.
    P: Palm branches at the altar mark our celebration.
    Scripture   Philippians 2:5-11
    Extinguishing Of The Sixth Lenten Candle
    Prayer
    Choral Introit

Good Friday
or The Passion Of Passion/Palm Sunday

Service Of The Lenten Candles   Reader: _____

    Choral Introit

    Litany   From Psalm 22:1, 28

    R: My God, my God, why have you forsaken me?

    P: We hear you, Christ.

    R: Why are you so far away?

    P: Who has really caused the distance?

    R: Won't you listen to my groans? Come to my rescue!

    P: You are in control, O God. You rule over all.

    Scripture   Hebrews 10:16-25

    Extinguishing Of The Christ Candle

    Prayer

    Choral Introit

Easter Sunday

Service Of The Christ Candle   Reader: _____

    Choral Introit

    Litany   From Psalm 16:7-10

    R: Praise God, for he has guided us through the night.

    P: God is always with us — as close as by our side.

    R: Let us rejoice and be glad! Even our physical bodies have hope.

    P: For God will not leave us in death — just as he has not left his Son in the tomb.

    Scripture   Colossians 3:1-4

    Extinguishing Of The Christ Candle

    Prayer

    Choral Introit

Words Of Introits For Year A

First Verse, All Sundays
We journey together this season of Lent;
A time to reflect, a time to forgive, a time to repent,
A time to remember, a time to recall
Christ's giving through suffering, his death and resurrection for all.

First Sunday In Lent
Romans 5:12-19
One candle not burning; this season we're in
Calls us to remember all we have done in this world of sin.
Our sin came from Adam and death brought the strife.
But through Christ the Son, his sacrifice done, gives eternal life.

Second Sunday In Lent
Romans 4:1-5, 13-17
Two candles not burning and we must proclaim
That Abraham's faith was righteous to God; we must be the same.
God loves and accepts us not for what we've done,
But through faith and trust our God accepts us through Jesus the Son.

Third Sunday In Lent
Romans 5:1-11
Three candles not burning. With spirit-filled hearts,
We suffer, endure and yet we are sure of what God imparts.
Christ died to redeem us. Our joy will increase
By ending all strife with eternal life and giving us peace.

Fourth Sunday In Lent
Ephesians 5:8-14
Four candles not burning makes darkness increase.
O God, make our light be burning so bright that darkness would cease.
We all would be sleeping and night would befall.
But then light would show up all that we know. Christ shine on us all!

Fifth Sunday In Lent
Romans 8:6-11
Five candles not burning. Our minds come to cry
For wants and desires that build up the fires that cause us to die.
As God's Holy Spirit rules over the strife,
The turmoils shall cease by bringing us peace and giving new life.

Passion/Palm Sunday
Philippians 2:5-11
Six candles not burning, recalling God's Son
Who came down to earth, was humbled at birth, was like everyone.
God gave him the honor; we share through the Word
So people can see; that all may agree that Jesus is Lord.

Good Friday
or The Passion Of Passion/Palm Sunday
Hebrews 10:16-25

No candles are burning. The time now is sure.
With the blood of Jesus, God now can free us; make our hearts pure.
Our sins are forgiven, our consciences free.
We now have the courage to worship God for eternity.

Easter Sunday
Colossians 3:1-4

We journeyed together this season of Lent.
We paused to reflect, reached out to forgive and strove to repent,
Took time to remember and then to recall
Christ's giving through suffering, his death and resurrection for all.

Sing out, alleluia! Sing out with one voice.
For what God has done through Jesus, his Son, sing out and rejoice!
The tomb now is empty without final breath.
The victory is won; new life is begun. Christ overcame death.

Year A — First Sunday In Lent

(Distribute this sheet to the readers.)

Date: _____

Reader A: _____   Reader B: _____

Choral Introit
(While the first verse of the choral introit is being sung, Readers A and B come forward and stand beside the Lenten candles. Reader B should bring a Bible.)

Litany   From Psalm 32:19-22
Reader A: Please turn to the Lenten litany in your bulletins:
           (Pause until the congregation is ready)
           We have a wonderful God!
           Those of us who honor and trust him can see all the blessings he has for us.
           Praise God for his great kindness.
           for he answers our cries for help.

Scripture
Reader B: Our scripture for this first Sunday in Lent is taken from Paul's letter to the Romans, chapter five, verses twelve through nineteen.
           (Then read Romans 5:12-19)

Extinguishing Of The First Lenten Candle
Reader A: As we extinguish the first Lenten candle, we are reminded that we all are in sin. But God's gift of Christ has made us acceptable to God and as a result, we can have eternal life. Even though sin ruled through death, God rules over all through Christ.
(While Reader A is speaking, Reader B takes the candle snuffer and extinguishes the first candle on the left.)

Prayer
Reader B: Let us pray: *(pause)* O God, we give you thanks, praise, and glory for your love and kindness shown through your Son, Jesus Christ. Help us this Lenten season to truly prepare our hearts for fellowship with you. Amen.

Choral Introit
(While the second verse of the choral introit is being sung, the readers may be seated.)

Note: Should one of the readers be unable to read, let one do the reading while the other extinguishes the light.

Lenten Introit

First Sunday in Lent - Year A
Romans 5:12-19

Robert S. Jarboe

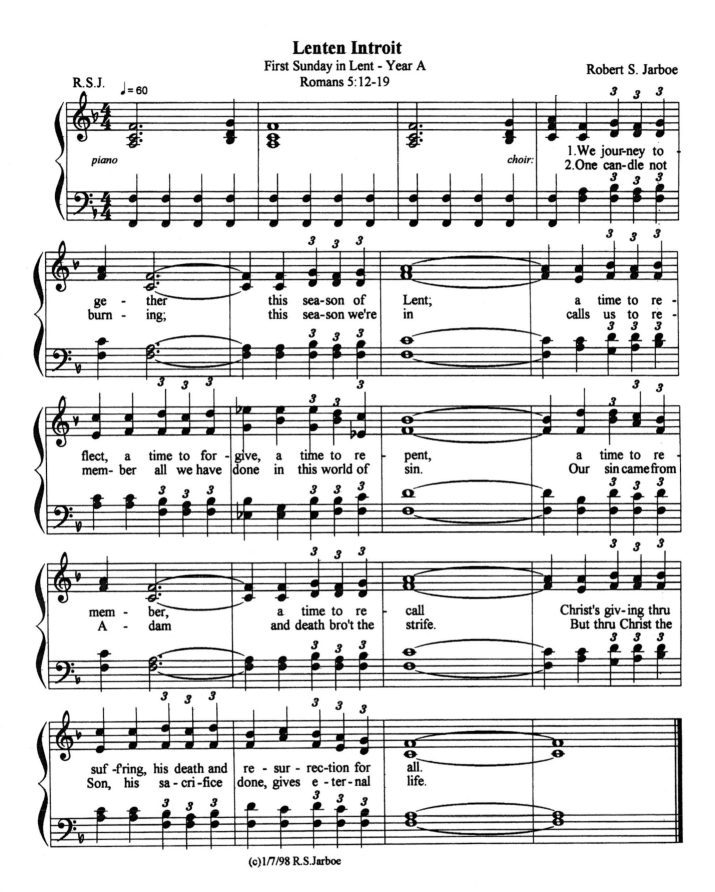

13

Year A — Second Sunday In Lent

(Distribute this sheet to the readers.)

Date: _____

Reader A: _____   Reader B: _____

Choral Introit
(While the first verse of the choral introit is being sung, Readers A and B come forward and stand beside the Lenten candles. Reader B should bring a Bible.)

Litany   From Psalm 121:1, 2, 8
Reader A: Please turn to the Lenten litany in your bulletins:
            (Pause until the congregation is ready)
            Where do we find help?
            All help comes from our Creator God.
            How much will God protect us?
            God will protect us always and everywhere.

Scripture
Reader B: Our scripture for this second Sunday in Lent is taken from Paul's letter to the Romans, chapter four, verses one through five and thirteen through seventeen.
            (Then read Romans 4:1-5, 13-17)

Extinguishing Of The Second Lenten Candle
Reader A: As we extinguish the second Lenten candle, we are reminded that we can never earn God's kindness. It can only be obtained through faith. This is a promise that was given to Abraham and his descendants. Therefore, this promise is for us as well.
(While Reader A is speaking, Reader B takes the candle snuffer and extinguishes the first candle on the right.)

Prayer
Reader B: Let us pray: *(pause)* O God, we do not deserve your kindness — but we say that based on who we are and what we have done. But your acceptance of us is based on our faith in you. Only then are we found worthy. Increase our faith, O Lord, our God, who redeems through Jesus Christ. Amen.

Choral Introit
(While the second verse of the choral introit is being sung, the readers may be seated.)

Note: Should one of the readers be unable to read, let one do the reading while the other extinguishes the light.

Lenten Introit

Second Sunday in Lent - Year A
Romans 4:1-5,13-17

Robert S. Jarboe

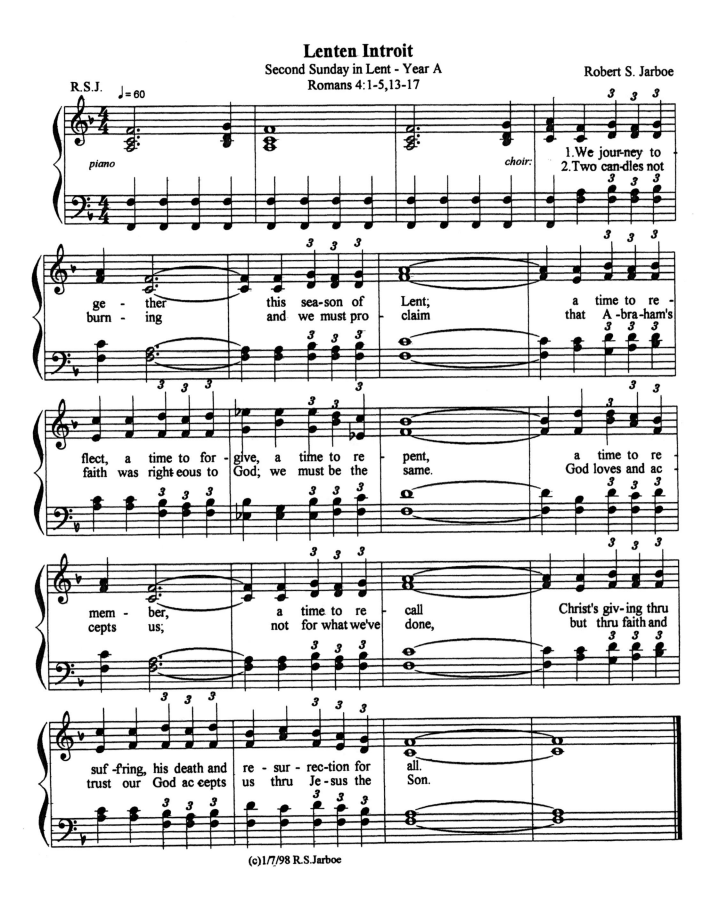

15

Year A — Third Sunday In Lent

(Distribute this sheet to the readers.)

Date: _____

Reader A: _____ Reader B: _____

Choral Introit
(While the first verse of the choral introit is being sung, Readers A and B come forward and stand beside the Lenten candles. Reader B should bring a Bible.)

Litany   From Psalm 95:2, 3, 7
Reader A: Please turn to the Lenten litany in your bulletins:
             (Pause until the congregation is ready)
             With thankful hearts, let us worship God.
             He is the greatest over all.
             We are the people of God.
             So we need to listen to him.

Scripture
Reader B: Our scripture for this third Sunday in Lent is taken from Paul's letter to the Romans, chapter five, verses
             one through eleven.
             (Then read Romans 5:1-11)

Extinguishing Of The Third Lenten Candle
Reader A: As we extinguish the third Lenten candle, we recall that we are not alone in our suffering. God under-
             stands. We need to learn how to endure in our suffering so that our hope will never waver in the light of
             God's love.
(While Reader A is speaking, Reader B takes the candle snuffer and extinguishes the second candle on the left.)

Prayer
Reader B: Let us pray: *(pause)* O God, sometimes it is too easy to give up in our suffering and spiritually walk
             away from you. Give us strength and confidence to endure so that through our hope your glory of eternal
             life may be realized. Amen.

Choral Introit
(While the second verse of the choral introit is being sung, the readers may be seated.)

Note: Should one of the readers be unable to read, let one do the reading while the other extinguishes the light.

Lenten Introit

Third Sunday in Lent - Year A
Romans 5:1-11

Robert S. Jarboe

Year A — Fourth Sunday In Lent

(Distribute this sheet to the readers.)

Date: _____

Reader A: _____ Reader B: _____

Choral Introit
(While the first verse of the choral introit is being sung, Readers A and B come forward and stand beside the Lenten candles. Reader B should bring a Bible.)

Litany From Psalm 23:1, 6

Reader A: Please turn to the Lenten litany in your bulletins:
(Pause until the congregation is ready)
God cares for us like a loving shepherd.
We find rest and refreshment.
God's love and kindness is always with us.
And we will live forever.

Scripture

Reader B: Our scripture for this fourth Sunday in Lent is taken from Paul's letter to the Ephesians, chapter five, verses eight through fourteen.
(Then read Ephesians 5:8-14.)

Extinguishing Of The Fourth Lenten Candle

Reader A: As we extinguish the fourth Lenten candle, we are reminded of the darkness of our lives. God calls us to be people of light — to live our lives so that there is nothing that needs to be hidden. Let us wake up and be a reflection of Christ's light. Amen.
(While Reader A is speaking, Reader B takes the candle snuffer and extinguishes the second candle on the right.)

Prayer

Reader B: Let us pray: *(pause)* O God, sometimes we feel there is comfort and security in darkness. But stir our spirits to realize the joy that is found in the light of Christ, for we know that there is nothing that can be hidden from you. Amen.

Choral Introit
(While the second verse of the choral introit is being sung, the readers may be seated.)

Note: Should one of the readers be unable to read, let one do the reading while the other extinguishes the light.

Lenten Introit

Fourth Sunday in Lent - Year A
Ephesians 5:8-14

Robert S. Jarboe

1.We jour-ney to ge-ther this sea-son of Lent; a time to re-flect, a time to for-give, a time to re-pent, a time to re-mem-ber, a time to re-call Christ's giv-ing thru suf-fring, his death and re-sur-rec-tion for all.

2.Four can-dles not burn-ing makes dark-ness in-crease. O God, make our light be burn-ing so bright that dark-ness would cease. We all would be sleep-ing and night would be-fall. But then light would show up all that we know. Christ shine on us all!

19

Year A — Fifth Sunday In Lent

(Distribute this sheet to the readers.)

Date: _____

Reader A: _____ Reader B: _____

Choral Introit
(While the first verse of the choral introit is being sung, Readers A and B come forward and stand beside the Lenten candles. Reader B should bring a Bible.)

Litany   From Psalm 130:4, 5, 7, 8
Reader A: Please turn to the Lenten litany in your bulletins:
          (Pause until the congregation is ready)
          We worship a forgiving God.
          And we wait and trust on his promises.
          Only God has the power to save — so trust him.
          We are saved from our wrongdoings.

Scripture
Reader B: Our scripture for this fifth Sunday in Lent is taken from Paul's letter to the Romans, chapter eight, verses six through eleven.
          (Then read Romans 8:6-11)

Extinguishing Of The Fifth Lenten Candle
Reader A: As we extinguish the fifth Lenten candle, we recall how our desires of the mind crowd out God's Holy Spirit. As a result, we deprive ourselves of God's gift of peace and new life. Through Christ, God came to give us that gift if we desire him instead of the things of the world.
(While Reader A is speaking, Reader B takes the candle snuffer and extinguishes the third candle on the left.)

Prayer
Reader B: Let us pray: *(pause)* O God, we realize that we get so caught up in the ways of the world that we forget your divine love and power. Help us to discover that wonderful divine peace that can only come from your Son, Jesus Christ. Amen.

Choral Introit
(While the second verse of the choral introit is being sung, the readers may be seated.)

Note: Should one of the readers be unable to read, let one do the reading while the other extinguishes the light.

Lenten Introit

Fifth Sunday in Lent - Year A
Romans 8:6-11

Robert S. Jarboe

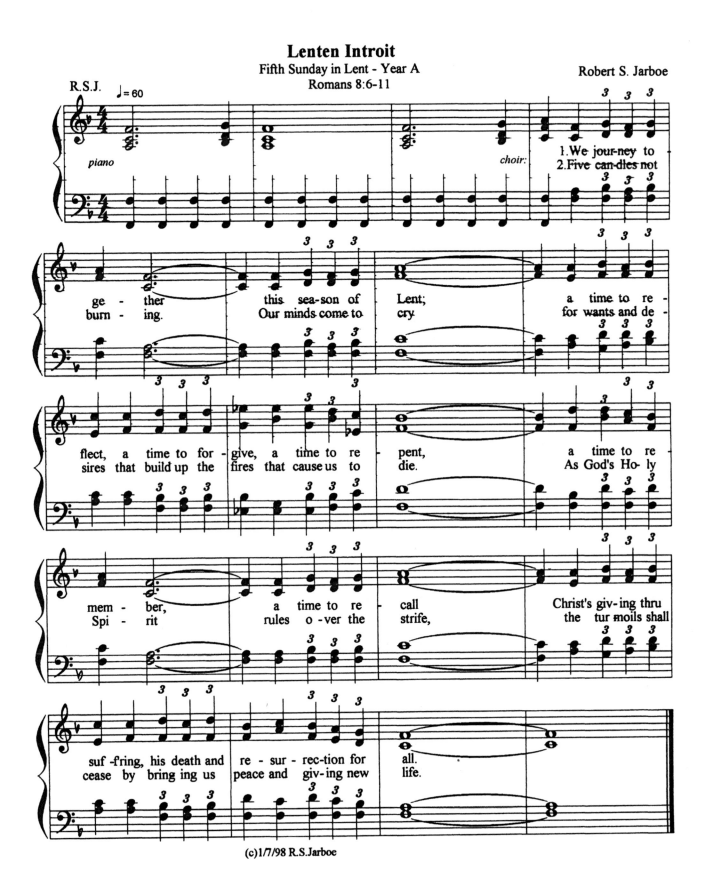

21

Year A — Passion/Palm Sunday

(Distribute this sheet to the readers.)

Date: _____

Reader A: _____   Reader B: _____

Choral Introit
(While the first verse of the choral introit is being sung, Readers A and B come forward and stand beside the Lenten candles. Reader B should bring a Bible.)

Litany   From Psalm 118:19, 20, 27
Reader A: Please turn to the Lenten litany in your bulletins:
               (Pause until the congregation is ready)
               Let us enter God's gates of justice with thankful hearts.
               Anyone who is right with God can enter.
               This is God's day to celebrate.
               Palm branches at the altar mark our celebration.

Scripture
Reader B: Our scripture for this Passion/Palm Sunday is taken from Paul's letter to the Philippians, chapter two, verses five through eleven.
               (Then read Philippians 2:5-11)

Extinguishing Of The Sixth Lenten Candle
Reader A: As we extinguish the sixth Lenten candle, we recall that God's Son, Jesus Christ, became like one of us so that we may have access to God and this became possible through Christ's death on the cross.
(While Reader A is speaking, Reader B takes the candle snuffer and extinguishes the third candle on the right.)

Prayer
Reader B: Let us pray: *(pause)* O God, what Christ has done for you and for us is truly wondrous. Even though he was your son, he humbled himself for us on the cross. We truly agree, "Jesus Christ is Lord!" Amen.

Choral Introit
(While the second verse of the choral introit is being sung, the readers may be seated.)

Note: Should one of the readers be unable to read, let one do the reading while the other extinguishes the light.

Lenten Introit

Palm/Passion Sunday - Year A
Philippians 2:5-11

Robert S. Jarboe

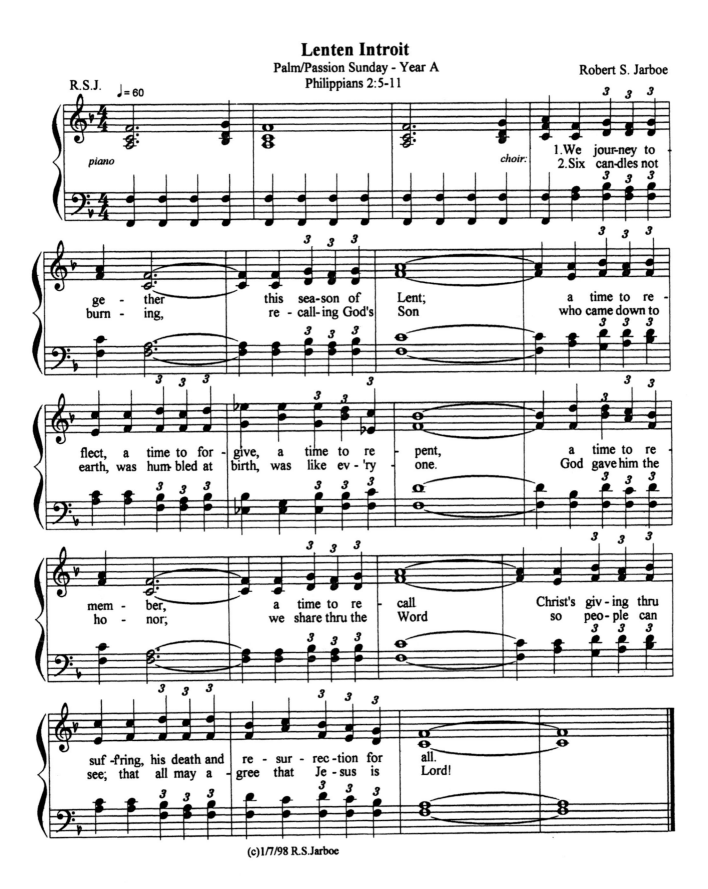

23

Year A — Good Friday
(Or the last half of Passion/Palm Sunday service)
(Distribute this sheet to the readers.)

Date: _____

Reader A: _____   Reader B: _____

Choral Introit
(While the first verse of the choral introit is being sung, Readers A and B come forward and stand beside the Lenten candles. Reader B should bring a Bible.)

Litany   From Psalm 22:1, 28
Reader A: Please turn to the Lenten litany in your bulletins:
            (Pause until the congregation is ready)
            My God, my God, why have you forsaken me?
            We hear you, Christ.
            Why are you so far away?
            Who has really caused the distance?
            Won't you listen to my groans? Come to my rescue!
            You are in control, O God. You rule over all.

Scripture
Reader B: Our scripture for this Good Friday *(or: for the Passion of this service)* is taken from Paul's letter to the Hebrews, chapter ten, verses sixteen through 25.
            (Then read Hebrews 10:16-25)

Extinguishing Of The Christ Candle
Reader A: As we extinguish the final Lenten candle, the Christ Candle, may we be humbled by what God has done for us through his Son, Jesus Christ. Until the great resurrection, we will be in darkness because of his death. But be in hope, for Christ's final victory will be soon.
(While Reader A is speaking, Reader B takes the candle snuffer and extinguishes the final candle that is lit.)

Prayer
Reader B: Let us pray: *(pause)* O God, this darkness is caused by what we have done and the only way that the true light can be returned is through your Son, Jesus Christ. Help our spirits retain the hope that Christ has overcome death — that Christ will conquer all — that our sins are forgiven — and that your Kingdom will truly be established. Amen.

Choral Introit
(While the second verse of the choral introit is being sung, the readers may be seated.)

Note: Should one of the readers be unable to read, let one do the reading while the other extinguishes the light.

Lenten Introit

Good Friday - Year A
Hebrews 10:16-25

Robert S. Jarboe

Year A — Easter Sunday

(Distribute this sheet to the readers.)

Date: _____

Reader A: _____   Reader B: _____

Choral Introit
(While the first verse of the choral introit is being sung, Readers A and B come forward and stand beside the Lenten candles. Reader B should bring a Bible.)

Litany   From Psalm 16:7-10
Reader A: Please turn to the litany in your bulletins:
(Pause until the congregation is ready)
Praise God, for he has guided us through the night.
God is always with us — as close as by our side.
Let us rejoice and be glad! Even our physical bodies have hope.
For God will not leave us in death — just as he has not left his Son in the tomb.

Scripture
Reader B: Our scripture for this Easter Sunday is taken from Paul's letter to the Colossians, chapter three, verses one through four.
(Then read Colossians 3:1-4)

Lighting Of The Christ Candle
Reader A: This morning we light the Christ Candle to remind us that in Christ is life and that life is the light for all people. The light has pierced the darkness and the darkness can never overtake the light — the one true Light which is found in Jesus Christ.
(While Reader A is speaking, Reader B takes the small candle and transfers the light from the altar candle to the Christ Candle.)

Prayer
Reader B: Let us pray: *(pause)* O God, we give you praise, honor, and glory for bringing us new life through your Son, Jesus Christ. We rejoice in knowing that we will rise from death like Christ and, in so doing, will live eternally with you. Amen.

Choral Introit
(While the second verse of the choral introit is being sung, the readers may be seated.)

Note: Should one of the readers be unable to read, let one do the reading while the other transfers the light.

Lenten Introit

Easter Sunday - Year A
Colossians 3:1-4

Robert S. Jarboe

Bulletin Inserts For Year B

(R - Reader; P - People)

First Sunday In Lent

Service Of The Lenten Candles   Reader: _____

    Choral Introit

    Litany   From Psalm 25:4, 5, 8

    R: Let us call upon the Lord to show us how to live.

    P: Show us the truth, O God, and teach us every day.

    R: Our God is good. Our God is sure.

    P: For he shows us the right way.

    Scripture   1 Peter 3:18-22

    Extinguishing Of The First Lenten Candle

    Prayer

    Choral Introit

Second Sunday In Lent

Service Of The Lenten Candles   Reader: _____

    Choral Introit

    Litany   From Psalm 22:24, 26

    R: The Lord does not ignore us or hide from us when we are troubled.

    P: God hears our every cry.

    R: Whatever we need, God will satisfy.

    P: Therefore, we give God the praise.

    Scripture   Romans 4:13-25

    Extinguishing Of The Second Lenten Candle

    Prayer

    Choral Introit

Third Sunday In Lent

Service Of The Lenten Candles   Reader: _____

    Choral Introit

    Litany   From Psalm 19:1, 2

    R: Every day as we face the creation of God

    P: we are reminded of what God has done.

    R: Day after day — night after night

    P: we are reminded of God's glory.

    Scripture   1 Corinthians 1:18-25

    Extinguishing Of The Third Lenten Candle

    Prayer

    Choral Introit

Fourth Sunday In Lent

Service Of The Lenten Candles   Reader: _____
    Choral Introit
    Litany   From Psalm 107:1, 22
    R: Give thanks for the goodness of God.
    P: For God's love is everlasting.
    R: Let us give of ourselves to show our thanksgiving.
    P: Let our joy proclaim what God has done through Jesus Christ.
    Scripture   Ephesians 2:1-10
    Extinguishing Of The Fourth Lenten Candle
    Prayer
    Choral Introit

Fifth Sunday In Lent

Service Of The Lenten Candles   Reader: _____
    Choral Introit
    Litany   From Psalm 51:7, 10
    R: It is time for our sins to be washed away
    P: that we may be as clean as the fresh-driven snow.
    R: May God make our hearts pure
    P: and our spirits right with him.
    Scripture   Hebrews 5:5-10
    Extinguishing Of The Fifth Lenten Candle
    Prayer
    Choral Introit

Passion/Palm Sunday

Service Of The Lenten Candles   Reader: _____
    Choral Introit
    Litany   From Psalm 118:19, 20, 27
    R: Let us enter God's gates of justice with thankful hearts.
    P: Anyone who is right with God can enter.
    R: This is God's day to celebrate.
    P: Palm branches at the altar mark our celebration.
    Scripture   Philippians 2:5-11
    Extinguishing Of The Sixth Lenten Candle
    Prayer
    Choral Introit

Good Friday
or The Passion of Passion/Palm Sunday

Service Of The Lenten Candles   Reader: _____

    Choral Introit

    Litany   From Psalm 22:1, 28

R: My God, my God, why have you forsaken me?

P: We hear you, Christ.

R: Why are you so far away?

P: Who has really caused the distance?

R: Won't you listen to my groans? Come to my rescue!

P: You are in control, O God. You rule over all.

    Scripture   Hebrews 10:16-25

    Extinguishing Of The Christ Candle

    Prayer

    Choral Introit

Easter Sunday

Service Of The Lenten Candles   Reader: _____

    Choral Introit

    Litany   From Psalm 16:7-10

R: Praise God, for he has guided us through the night.

P: God is always with us — as close as by our side.

R: Let us rejoice and be glad! Even our physical bodies have hope.

P: For God will not leave us in death — just as he has not left his Son in the tomb.

    Scripture   1 Corinthians 15:1-11

    Lighting Of The Christ Candle

    Prayer

    Choral Introit

Words Of Introits For Year B

First Verse, All Sundays
We journey together this season of Lent;
A time to reflect, a time to forgive, a time to repent,
A time to remember, a time to recall
Christ's giving through suffering, his death and resurrection for all.

First Sunday In Lent
1 Peter 3:18-22
One candle not burning. This season we're in,
We think of the death through Christ's final breath to pay for each sin.
For those who are guilty, he was crucified,
But then was raised up from his suffering cup and is at God's side.

Second Sunday In Lent
Romans 4:13-25
Two candles not burning. With Abraham's call,
A promise received; because he believed, he's father of all.
We, too, are accepted as Christ enters in.
For death on the cross has taken our loss; redeemed us from sin.

Third Sunday In Lent
1 Corinthians 1:18-25
Three candles not burning. The wisdom of men
In time will be lost to learn of the cross. They won't understand.
For what is the message to those who hear then?
The foolish and weak which no one will seek is better than men.

Fourth Sunday In Lent
Ephesians 2:1-10
Four candles not burning. The ways of the world
By spirit are dead when we should, instead, repent to the Lord.
Then God in his mercy and great in his love
Will save us by grace and give us a place in heaven above.

Fifth Sunday In Lent
Hebrews 5:5-10
Five candles not burning. Christ chosen to be,
"For you are my Son; I, Father, we're one for eternity."
God gives his salvation to all who obey.
The suffering Son, but what he has done, death's taken away.

Passion/Palm Sunday
Philippians 2:5-11
Six candles, not burning, recalling God's Son
Who came down to earth, was humbled at birth, was like everyone.
God gave him the honor; we share through the Word
So people can see; that all may agree that Jesus is Lord!

Good Friday
or The Passion Of Passion/Palm Sunday
Hebrews 10:16-25

No candles are burning. The time now is sure.
With the blood of Jesus, God now can free us; make our hearts pure.
Our sins are forgiven; our consciences free.
We now have the courage to worship God for eternity.

Easter Sunday
1 Corinthians 15:1-11

We journeyed together this season of Lent.
We paused to reflect, reached out to forgive and strove to repent,
Took time to remember and then to recall
Christ's giving through suffering, his death and resurrection for all.

Sing out, alleluia! Sing out with one voice.
For what God has done through Jesus, his Son, sing out and rejoice!
The tomb now is empty without final breath.
The victory is won; new life is begun. Christ overcame death.

Year B — First Sunday In Lent

(Distribute this sheet to the readers.)

Date: _____

Reader A: _____   Reader B: _____

Choral Introit
(While the first verse of the choral introit is being sung, Readers A and B come forward and stand beside the Lenten candles. Reader B should bring a Bible.)

Litany   From Psalm 25:4, 5, 8

Reader A: Please turn to the Lenten litany in your bulletins:
(Pause until the congregation is ready)
Let us call on God to show us how to live.
Show us the truth, O God, and teach us every day.
Our God is good. Our God is sure.
For he shows us the right way.

Scripture

Reader B: Our scripture for this first Sunday in Lent is taken from first Peter, chapter three, verses eighteen through 22.
(Then read 1 Peter 3:18-22)

Extinguishing Of The First Lenten Candle

Reader A: As we extinguish the first Lenten candle, we are reminded that when the body of Christ was killed, he was made alive in the Spirit and preached to the imprisoned spirits to set them free. As in the time of Noah when God waited patiently for his people, God also waits for us to turn to him. In so doing, we will be washed clean and be made right with him — this is his promise to us.
(While Reader A is speaking, Reader B takes the candle snuffer and extinguishes the first candle on the left.)

Prayer

Reader B: Let us pray: *(pause)* O God, we rejoice in that as you saved Noah and his family through the flood, you also save all those who turn to you in baptism. Give us strength and courage to turn to you with repentant hearts that we may be saved. Amen.

Choral Introit
(While the second verse of the choral introit is being sung, the readers may be seated.)

Note: Should one of the readers be unable to read, let one do the reading while the other extinguishes the light.

Lenten Introit

First Sunday in Lent - Year B
1 Peter 3:18-22

Robert S. Jarboe

35

Year B — Second Sunday In Lent

(Distribute this sheet to the readers.)

Date: _____

Reader A: _____   Reader B: _____

Choral Introit
(While the first verse of the choral introit is being sung, Readers A and B come forward and stand beside the Lenten candles. Reader B should bring a Bible.)

Litany   From Psalm 22:24, 26
Reader A: Please turn to the Lenten litany in your bulletins:
(Pause until the congregation is ready)
The Lord does not ignore us or hide from us when we are troubled.
God hears our every cry.
Whatever we need, God will satisfy.
Therefore, we give God the praise.

Scripture
Reader B: Our scripture for this second Sunday in Lent is taken from Paul's letter to the Romans, chapter four, verses thirteen through 25.
(Then read Romans 4:13-25)

Extinguishing Of The Second Lenten Candle
Reader A: As we extinguish the second Lenten candle, we are reminded of God's promise to Abraham and Abraham's faithful trust in God. God's promise to us, if we believe, is that we will be accepted by him. What is it we believe? We believe that Jesus died for our sins and was raised up from death so we can be right with God. Praise God for his matchless gift!
(While Reader A is speaking, Reader B takes the candle snuffer and extinguishes the first candle on the right.)

Prayer
Reader B: Let us pray: *(pause)* O God, because of Abraham's faith and trust in you, you made him the father of all nations. You have made wonderful promises for us as well. We proclaim our belief, but help us in our unbelief. Amen.

Choral Introit
(While the second verse of the choral introit is being sung, the readers may be seated.)

Note: Should one of the readers be unable to read, let one do the reading while the other extinguishes the light.

Lenten Introit

Second Sunday in Lent - Year B
Romans 4:13-25

Robert S. Jarboe

1. We journey together this season of Lent; a time to reflect, a time to forgive, a time to repent, a time to remember, a time to recall Christ's giving thru suffring, his death and resurrection for all.

2. Two candles not burning. With Abraham's call, a promise received; because he believed, he's father of all. We, too, are accepted as Christ enters in. For death on the cross has taken our loss; redeemed us from sin.

(c)1/7/98 R.S.Jarboe

37

Year B — Third Sunday In Lent

(Distribute this sheet to the readers.)

Date: _____

Reader A: _____   Reader B: _____

Choral Introit
(While the first verse of the choral introit is being sung, Readers A and B come forward and stand beside the Lenten candles. Reader B should bring a Bible.)

Litany
From Psalm 19:1, 2

Reader A: Please turn to the Lenten litany in your bulletins:
(Pause until the congregation is ready)
Every day as we face the creation of God
we are reminded of what God has done.
Day after day — night after night
we are reminded of God's glory.

Scripture
Reader B: Our scripture for this third Sunday in Lent is taken from Paul's first letter to the Corinthians, chapter one, verses eighteen through 25.
(Then read 1 Corinthians 1:18-25)

Extinguishing Of The Third Lenten Candle
Reader A: As we extinguish the third Lenten candle, we are reminded that though we believe that we may be wise, we are only foolish in the eyes of God. To get even a small understanding of the mind of God, we need to understand the meaning of the cross. In so doing, we realize that even God's foolishness is wiser than all men.
(While Reader A is speaking, Reader B takes the candle snuffer and extinguishes the second candle on the left.)

Prayer
Reader B: Let us pray: *(pause)* O God, we are so foolish when we believe that we have all the answers to the problems of this world. As we begin to understand the meaning of the cross, help us to see that it is only possible through your power. Amen.

Choral Introit
(While the second verse of the choral introit is being sung, the readers may be seated.)

Note: Should one of the readers be unable to read, let one do the reading while the other extinguishes the light.

Lenten Introit

Third Sunday in Lent - Year B
1 Corinthians 1:18-25

Robert S. Jarboe

Year B — Fourth Sunday In Lent

(Distribute this sheet to the readers.)

Date: _____

Reader A: _____   Reader B: _____

Choral Introit
(While the first verse of the choral introit is being sung, Readers A and B come forward and stand beside the Lenten candles. Reader B should bring a Bible.)

Litany
From Psalm 107:1, 22

Reader A: Please turn to the Lenten litany in your bulletins:
(Pause until the congregation is ready)
Give thanks for the goodness of God.
For God's love is everlasting.
Let us give of ourselves to show our thanksgiving.
Let our joy proclaim what God has done through Jesus Christ.

Scripture
Reader B: Our scripture for this fourth Sunday in Lent is taken from Paul's letter to the Ephesians, chapter two, verses one through ten.
(Then read Ephesians 2:1-10)

Extinguishing Of The Fourth Lenten Candle
Reader A: As we extinguish the fourth Lenten candle, we are reminded that though we were spiritually dead, God has given us new life through Jesus Christ. Despite all the wrong we have done against God, God has forgiven us through his grace as long as we believe in him.
(While Reader A is speaking, Reader B takes the candle snuffer and extinguishes the second candle on the right.)

Prayer
Reader B: Let us pray: *(pause)* O God, we can never imagine how great your love is for us, how through your grace you care for us. We can never make ourselves right with you. Only you can do that and we give you the praise and glory for your grace and love that makes it possible. Amen.

Choral Introit
(While the second verse of the choral introit is being sung, the readers may be seated.)

Note: Should one of the readers be unable to read, let one do the reading while the other extinguishes the light.

Lenten Introit

Fourth Sunday in Lent - Year B

Ephesians 2:1-10

Robert S. Jarboe

Year B — Fifth Sunday In Lent

(Distribute this sheet to the readers.)

Date: _____

Reader A: _____   Reader B: _____

Choral Introit
(While the first verse of the choral introit is being sung, Readers A and B come forward and stand beside the Lenten candles. Reader B should bring a Bible.)

Litany
From Psalm 51:7, 10

Reader A: Please turn to the Lenten litany in your bulletins:
(Pause until the congregation is ready)
It is time for our sins to be washed away
that we may be as clean as the fresh-driven snow.
May God make our hearts pure
and our spirits right with him.

Scripture
Reader B: Our scripture for this fifth Sunday in Lent is taken from Paul's letter to the Hebrews, chapter five, verses five through ten.
(Then read Hebrews 5:5-10)

Extinguishing Of The Fifth Lenten Candle
Reader A: As we extinguish the fifth Lenten candle, we are reminded that Christ is the great high priest chosen by God. Through his suffering he learned to obey God and his eternal salvation is for us as well if we obey.
(While Reader A is speaking, Reader B takes the candle snuffer and extinguishes the third candle on the left.)

Prayer
Reader B: Let us pray: *(pause)* O God, help us to realize that the only true good we can do in this world is by obeying you. By being obedient to the perfect high priest. Jesus Christ, we know that you promise us eternal salvation. We give you praise. Amen.

Choral Introit
(While the second verse of the choral introit is being sung, the readers may be seated.)

Note: Should one of the readers be unable to read, let one do the reading while the other extinguishes the light.

Lenten Introit

Fifth Sunday in Lent - Year B
Hebrews 5:5-10

Robert S. Jarboe

Year B — Passion/Palm Sunday

(Distribute this sheet to the readers.)

Date: _____

Reader A: _____   Reader B: _____

Choral Introit
(While the first verse of the choral introit is being sung, Readers A and B come forward and stand beside the Lenten candles. Reader B should bring a Bible.)

Litany   From Psalm 118:19, 20, 27
Reader A: Please turn to the Lenten litany in your bulletins:
(Pause until the congregation is ready)
Let us enter God's gates of justice with thankful hearts.
Anyone who is right with God can enter.
This is God's day to celebrate.
Palm branches at the altar mark our celebration.

Scripture
Reader B: Our scripture for this Passion/Palm Sunday is taken from Paul's letter to the Philippians, chapter two, verses five through eleven.
(Then read Philippians 2:5-11)

Extinguishing Of The Sixth Lenten Candle
Reader A: As we extinguish the sixth Lenten candle, we recall that God's Son, Jesus Christ, became like one of us so that we may have access to God and this became possible through Christ's death on the cross.
(While Reader A is speaking, Reader B takes the candle snuffer and extinguishes the third candle on the right.)

Prayer
Reader B: Let us pray: *(pause)* O God, what Christ has done for you and for us is truly wondrous. Even though he was your son, he humbled himself for us on the cross. We truly agree, "Jesus Christ is Lord!" Amen.

Choral Introit
(While the second verse of the choral introit is being sung, the readers may be seated.)

Note: Should one of the readers be unable to read, let one do the reading while the other extinguishes the light.

Lenten Introit

Palm/Passion Sunday - Year B
Philippians 2:5-11

Robert S. Jarboe

Year B — Good Friday
(Or the last half of Passion/Palm Sunday service)
(Distribute this sheet to the readers.)

Date: _____

Reader A: _____   Reader B: _____

Choral Introit
(While the first verse of the choral introit is being sung, Readers A and B come forward and stand beside the Lenten candles. Reader B should bring a Bible.)

Litany   From Psalm 22:1, 28
Reader A: Please turn to the Lenten litany in your bulletins:
            (Pause until the congregation is ready)
            My God, my God, why have you forsaken me?
            We hear you, Christ.
            Why are you so far away?
            Who has really caused the distance?
            Won't you listen to my groans? Come to my rescue!
            You are in control, O God. You rule over all.

Scripture
Reader B: Our scripture for this Good Friday (*or: for the Passion of this service*) is taken from Paul's letter to the Hebrews, chapter ten, verses sixteen through 25.
            (Then read Hebrews 10:16-25)

Extinguishing Of The Christ Candle
Reader A: As we extinguish the final Lenten candle, the Christ Candle, may we be humbled by what God has done for us through his Son, Jesus Christ. Until the great resurrection, we will be in darkness because of his death. But be in hope, for Christ's final victory will be soon.
(While Reader A is speaking, Reader B takes the candle snuffer and extinguishes the final candle that is lit.)

Prayer
Reader B: Let us pray: *(pause)* O God, this darkness is caused by what we have done and the only way that the true light can be returned is through your Son, Jesus Christ. Help our spirits retain the hope that Christ has overcome death — that Christ will conquer all — that our sins are forgiven — and that your Kingdom will truly be established. Amen.

Choral Introit
(While the second verse of the choral introit is being sung, the readers may be seated.)

Note: Should one of the readers be unable to read, let one do the reading while the other extinguishes the light.

Lenten Introit

Good Friday - Year B

Hebrews 10:16-25

Robert S. Jarboe

47

Year B — Easter Sunday

(Distribute this sheet to the readers.)

Date: _____

Reader A: _____   Reader B: _____

Choral Introit
(While the first verse of the choral introit is being sung, Readers A and B come forward and stand beside the Lenten candles. Reader B should bring a Bible.)

Litany   From Psalm 16:7-10
Reader A: Please turn to the litany in your bulletins:
　　　　　　　(Pause until the congregation is ready)
　　　　　　　Praise God, for he has guided us through the night.
　　　　　　　God is always with us — as close as by our side.
　　　　　　　Let us rejoice and be glad! Even our physical bodies have hope.
　　　　　　　For God will not leave us in death — just as he has not left his Son in the tomb.

Scripture
Reader B: Our scripture for this Easter Sunday is taken from Paul's first letter to the Corinthians, chapter fifteen, verses one through eleven.
　　　　　　　(Then read 1 Corinthians 15:1-11)

Lighting Of The Christ Candle
Reader A: This morning we light the Christ Candle to remind us that in Christ is life and that life is the light for all people. The light has pierced the darkness and the darkness can never overtake the light — the one true Light which is found in Jesus Christ.
(While Reader A is speaking, Reader B takes the small candle and transfers the light from the altar candle to the Christ Candle.)

Prayer
Reader B: Let us pray: *(pause)* O God, we give you praise, honor, and glory for bringing us new life through your Son, Jesus Christ. We rejoice in knowing that we will rise from death like Christ and, in so doing, will live eternally with you. Amen.

Choral Introit
(While the second verse of the choral introit is being sung, the readers may be seated.)

Note: Should one of the readers be unable to read, let one do the reading while the other transfers the light.

Lenten Introit

Easter Sunday - Year B
1 Corinthians 15:1-11

Robert S. Jarboe

1. We journeyed together this sea-son of Lent. We paused to re-flect, reached out to for-give and strove to re-pent, took time to re-mem-ber and then to re-call with-out fi-nal breath.

2. Sing out, al-le-lu - ia! Sing out with one voice. For what God has done thru Je-sus, his Son, sing out and re-joice! The tomb now is emp-ty, Christ's giv-ing thru suf-fring, his death and re-sur-rec-tion for all.

The vic-t'ry is won; new life is be-gun. Christ o-ver-came death.

Bulletin Inserts For Year C

(R - Reader; P - People)

First Sunday In Lent

Service Of The Lenten Candles   Reader: _____
    Choral Introit
    Litany   From Psalm 91:1, 15
    R: All those who find their protection from God
    P: will find rest and assurance.
    R: All those who love God and call upon him for help
    P: will be answered and rescued.
    Scripture   Romans 10:8b-13
    Extinguishing Of The First Lenten Candle
    Prayer
    Choral Introit

Second Sunday In Lent

Service Of The Lenten Candles   Reader: _____
    Choral Introit
    Litany   From Psalm 27:13, 14
    R: Let us speak with confidence:
    P: We will see God's goodness all around us.
    R: We need to wait on God — to discover what God wants us to do.
    P: As we wait, our confidence will be strong and we will trust God.
    Scripture   Philippians 3:17—4:1
    Extinguishing Of The Second Lenten Candle
    Prayer
    Choral Introit

Third Sunday In Lent

Service Of The Lenten Candles   Reader: _____
    Choral Introit
    Litany   From Psalm 63:2, 3, 8
    R: Have we seen the power and glory of God?
    P: Does God's love mean more than life to us?
    R: We must stay close to God
    P: so that we may be supported by him.
    Scripture   1 Corinthians 10:1-13
    Extinguishing Of The Third Lenten Candle
    Prayer
    Choral Introit

Fourth Sunday In Lent

Service Of The Lenten Candles   Reader: _____
    Choral Introit
    Litany   From Psalm 32:1, 10
    R: We are surely a blessed people
    P: for God forgives us of our sins!
    R: As they are wiped away, God's kindness shields us.
    P: All of us who trust God are shielded.
    Scripture   2 Corinthians 5:16-21
    Extinguishing Of The Fourth Lenten Candle
    Prayer
    Choral Introit

Fifth Sunday In Lent

Service Of The Lenten Candles   Reader: _____
    Choral Introit
    Litany   From Psalm 126:4-6
    R: We should continually ask for God's blessings
    P: because like a desert stream, we are thirsty.
    R: We struggle in planting seeds of love and faith,
    P: but we rejoice as we see God multiplying what we have sown.
    Scripture   Philippians 3:4b-14
    Extinguishing Of The Fifth Lenten Candle
    Prayer
    Choral Introit

Passion/Palm Sunday

Service Of The Lenten Candles   Reader: _____
    Choral Introit
    Litany   From Psalm 118:19, 20, 27
    R: Let us enter God's gates of justice with thankful hearts.
    P: Anyone who is right with God can enter.
    R: This is God's day to celebrate.
    P: Palm branches at the altar mark our celebration.
    Scripture   Philippians 2:5-11
    Extinguishing Of The Sixth Lenten Candle
    Prayer
    Choral Introit

Good Friday
or The Passion of Passion/Palm Sunday

Service Of The Lenten Candles   Reader: _____

    Choral Introit

    Litany   From Psalm 22:1, 28

    R: My God, my God, why have you forsaken me?

    P: We hear you, Christ.

    R: Why are you so far away?

    P: Who has really caused the distance?

    R: Won't you listen to my groans? Come to my rescue!

    P: You are in control, O God. You rule over all.

    Scripture   Hebrews 10:16-25

    Extinguishing Of The Christ Candle

    Prayer

    Choral Introit

Easter Sunday

Service Of The Lenten Candles   Reader: _____

    Choral Introit

    Litany   From Psalm 16:7-10

    R: Praise God, for he has guided us through the night.

    P: God is always with us — as close as by our side.

    R: Let us rejoice and be glad! Even our physical bodies have hope.

    P: For God will not leave us in death — just as he has not left his Son in the tomb.

    Scripture   1 Corinthians 15:19-26

    Lighting Of The Christ Candle

    Prayer

    Choral Introit

Words Of Introits For Year C

First Verse, All Sundays
We journey together this season of Lent;
A time to reflect, a time to forgive, a time to repent,
A time to remember, a time to recall
Christ's giving through suffering, his death and resurrection for all.

First Sunday In Lent
Romans 10:8b-13
One candle not burning as we must perceive
That God is our fortress and he will save us if we believe.
We come and we worship; proclaim him as Lord.
And he will give safety in time of trouble as his reward.

Second Sunday In Lent
Philippians 3:17—4:1
Two candles not burning, we call on God's name
To help us reject those things of the world that bring us to shame.
Our place is in heaven; our Savior is there
Proclaiming his power, we will be like him, we must not despair.

Third Sunday In Lent
1 Corinthians 10:1-13
Three candles not burning, God, show us the way
By helping us trust you, as we must face temptations each day.
May we stand beside you; may we never fall.
May we never test you; whate'er we do, your name may we call.

Fourth Sunday In Lent
2 Corinthians 5:16-21
Four candles not burning and we must proclaim
God's love and forgiveness for all God's people; always the same.
God wants us to listen and not judge with ease.
The past is forgotten; everything's new; we must live in peace.

Fifth Sunday In Lent
Philippians 3:4b-14
Five candles not burning; we've not yet arrived
In running and struggling, reaching for heaven which we have strived.
For all that has value, now is of no worth
When counting the cost which Christ's life was lost; of coming to earth.

Passion/Palm Sunday
Philippians 2:5-11
Six candles, not burning, recalling God's Son
Who came down to earth, was humbled at birth, was like everyone.
God gave him the honor; we share through the Word
So people can see; that all may agree that Jesus is Lord!

Good Friday
or The Passion Of Passion/Palm Sunday
Hebrews 10:16-25

No candles are burning. The time now is sure.

With the blood of Jesus, God now can free us; make our hearts pure.

Our sins are forgiven; our consciences free.

We now have the courage to worship God for eternity.

Easter Sunday
1 Corinthians 15:19-26

We journeyed together this season of Lent.

We paused to reflect, reached out to forgive and strove to repent,

Took time to remember and then to recall

Christ's giving through suffering, his death and resurrection for all.

Sing out, alleluia! Sing out with one voice.

For what God has done through Jesus, his Son, sing out and rejoice!

The tomb now is empty without final breath.

The victory is won; new life is begun. Christ overcame death.

Year C — First Sunday In Lent

(Distribute this sheet to the readers.)

Date: _____

Reader A: _____   Reader B: _____

Choral Introit
(While the first verse of the choral introit is being sung, Readers A and B come forward and stand beside the Lenten candles. Reader B should bring a Bible.)

Litany
From Psalm 91:1, 15

Reader A: Please turn to the Lenten litany in your bulletins:
(Pause until the congregation is ready)
All those who find their protection from God
will find rest and assurance.
All those who love God and call upon him for help
will be answered and rescued.

Scripture
Reader B: Our scripture for this first Sunday in Lent is taken from Paul's letter to the Romans, chapter ten, the last half of verse eight through verse thirteen.
(Then read Romans 10:8b-13)

Extinguishing Of The First Lenten Candle
Reader A: As we extinguish the first Lenten candle, we recall how we vainly try to save ourselves, believing that we are God. May we be reminded of our shortsightedness so that we may truly believe in the one and only true God who can save us — the One who sent his Son, Jesus Christ — our Redeemer.
(While Reader A is speaking, Reader B takes the candle snuffer and extinguishes the first candle on the left.)

Prayer
Reader B: Let us pray: *(pause)* O God, as we are in this time of Lent, remind us of your generous and gracious love for all who believe in you, that all who proclaim "Jesus is Lord" will truly be saved. Amen.

Choral Introit
(While the second verse of the choral introit is being sung, the readers may be seated.)

Note: Should one of the readers be unable to read, let one do the reading while the other extinguishes the light.

Lenten Introit

First Sunday in Lent - Year C

Romans 10:8b-13

Robert S. Jarboe

Year C — Second Sunday In Lent

(Distribute this sheet to the readers.)

Date: _____

Reader A: _____   Reader B: _____

Choral Introit
(While the first verse of the choral introit is being sung, Readers A and B come forward and stand beside the Lenten candles. Reader B should bring a Bible.)

Litany
From Psalm 27:13, 14

Reader A: Please turn to the Lenten litany in your bulletins:
(Pause until the congregation is ready)
Let us speak with confidence:
We will see God's goodness all around us.
We need to wait on God — to discover what God wants us to do.
As we wait, our confidence will be strong and we will trust God.

Scripture
Reader B: Our scripture for this second Sunday in Lent is taken from Paul's letter to the Philippians, chapter three, verses seventeen through chapter fourteen, verse one.
(Then read Philippians 3:17—14:1)

Extinguishing Of The Second Lenten Candle
Reader A: We extinguish the second Lenten candle — reminding us of the things of the world that entice us away from God. May we keep our eyes on God, who has shown us his love through his Son, Jesus Christ.
(While Reader A is speaking, Reader B takes the candle snuffer and extinguishes the first candle on the right.)

Prayer
Reader B: Let us pray: *(pause)* O God, help us to comprehend that this world we live in is not everlasting. But you call us to prepare ourselves for your Kingdom which is truly everlasting. Amen.

Choral Introit
(While the second verse of the choral introit is being sung, the readers may be seated.)

Note: Should one of the readers be unable to read, let one do the reading while the other extinguishes the light.

Lenten Introit

Second Sunday in Lent - Year C
Philippians 3:17-4:1

Robert S. Jarboe

Year C — Third Sunday In Lent

(Distribute this sheet to the readers.)

Date: _____

Reader A: _____   Reader B: _____

Choral Introit
(While the first verse of the choral introit is being sung, Readers A and B come forward and stand beside the Lenten candles. Reader B should bring a Bible.)

Litany   From Psalm 63:2, 3, 8
Reader A: Please turn to the Lenten litany in your bulletins:
　　　　　　(Pause until the congregation is ready)
　　　　　　Have we seen the power and glory of God?
　　　　　　Does God's love mean more than life to us?
　　　　　　We must stay close to God
　　　　　　so that we may be supported by him.

Scripture
Reader B: Our scripture for this third Sunday in Lent is taken from Paul's first letter to the Corinthians, chapter ten, verses one through thirteen.
　　　　　　(Then read 1 Corinthians 10:1-13)

Extinguishing Of The Third Lenten Candle
Reader A: As we extinguish the third Lenten candle, we know that we face temptations every day. May we be reminded that if we should ever stumble and fall in our temptations, God's grace and love is always there to redeem us. This is only possible through his Son, Jesus Christ.
(While Reader A is speaking, Reader B takes the candle snuffer and extinguishes the second candle on the left.)

Prayer
Reader B: Let us pray: *(pause)* O God, may we never give up hope during those times that we fall away from your grace. But may we know that each time we turn to you, you are always present to renew and refresh our spirits. Amen.

Choral Introit
(While the second verse of the choral introit is being sung, the readers may be seated.)

Note: Should one of the readers be unable to read, let one do the reading while the other extinguishes the light.

Lenten Introit

Third Sunday in Lent - Year C
1 Corinthians 10:1-13

Robert S. Jarboe

61

Year C — Fourth Sunday In Lent

(Distribute this sheet to the readers.)

Date: _____

Reader A: _____   Reader B: _____

Choral Introit
(While the first verse of the choral introit is being sung, Readers A and B come forward and stand beside the Lenten candles. Reader B should bring a Bible.)

Litany
From Psalm 32:1, 10

Reader A: Please turn to the Lenten litany in your bulletins:
(Pause until the congregation is ready)
We are surely a blessed people
for God forgives us of our sins!
As they are wiped away, God's kindness shields us.
All of us who trust God are shielded.

Scripture
Reader B: Our scripture for this fourth Sunday in Lent is taken from Paul's second letter to the Corinthians, chapter five, verses sixteen through 21.
(Then read 2 Corinthians 5:16-21)

Extinguishing Of The Fourth Lenten Candle
Reader A: As we extinguish the fourth Lenten candle, we are reminded how easy it is to judge others who are not like us. We must remember that Christ, who was sinless, was judged in the very same manner. We must never forget that as God has made us acceptable through Christ, that offer is made for everyone as well.
(While Reader A is speaking, Reader B takes the candle snuffer and extinguishes the second candle on the right.)

Prayer
Reader B: Let us pray: *(pause)* O God, how easy it is to judge others who do not think as we do. Help us as your people to offer peace and forgiveness to all — not judgment. For this reason, Christ died. And this is our work for which you have called us. Amen.

Choral Introit
(While the second verse of the choral introit is being sung, the readers may be seated.)

Note: Should one of the readers be unable to read, let one do the reading while the other extinguishes the light.

Lenten Introit

Fourth Sunday in Lent - Year C
2 Corinthians 5:16-21

Robert S. Jarboe

1.We jour-ney to ge - ther this sea-son of Lent; a time to re - flect, a time to for - give, a time to re - pent, a time to re - mem - ber, a time to re - call Christ's giv - ing thru suf - f'ring, his death and re - sur - rec -tion for all.

2.Four can-dles not burn - ing and we must pro - claim God's love and for - give - ness for all God's peo - ple: al -ways the same. God wants us to list - en and not judge with ease. The past is for - got - ten; ev - 'ry thing's new; we must live in peace.

Year C — Fifth Sunday In Lent

(Distribute this sheet to the readers.)

Date: _____

Reader A: _____   Reader B: _____

Choral Introit
(While the first verse of the choral introit is being sung, Readers A and B come forward and stand beside the Lenten candles. Reader B should bring a Bible.)

Litany   From Psalm 126:4-6
Reader A: Please turn to the Lenten litany in your bulletins:
            (Pause until the congregation is ready)
            We should continually ask for God's blessings
            because like a desert stream, we are thirsty.
            We struggle in planting seeds of love and faith,
            but we rejoice as we see God multiplying what we have sown.

Scripture
Reader B: Our scripture for this fifth Sunday in Lent is taken from Paul's letter to the Philippians, chapter three, the last half of verse four through verse fourteen.
            (Then read Philippians 3:4b-14)

Extinguishing Of The Fifth Lenten Candle
Reader A: As we extinguish the fifth Lenten candle, we recall all those things that have value to us — those things which take our time and money to preserve. God has shown to us that everything is worthless compared to what Christ, his Son, has done for us.
(While Reader A is speaking, Reader B takes the candle snuffer and extinguishes the third candle on the left.)

Prayer
Reader B: Let us pray: *(pause)* O God, as we run the race, help us to keep our focus on the true prize — your Son, Jesus Christ. Help us to forget our past struggles so that we may persevere to accomplish the race you have set before us. Amen.

Choral Introit
(While the second verse of the choral introit is being sung, the readers may be seated.)

Note: Should one of the readers be unable to read, let one do the reading while the other extinguishes the light.

Lenten Introit

Fifth Sunday in Lent - Year C
Philippians 3:4b-14

Robert S. Jarboe

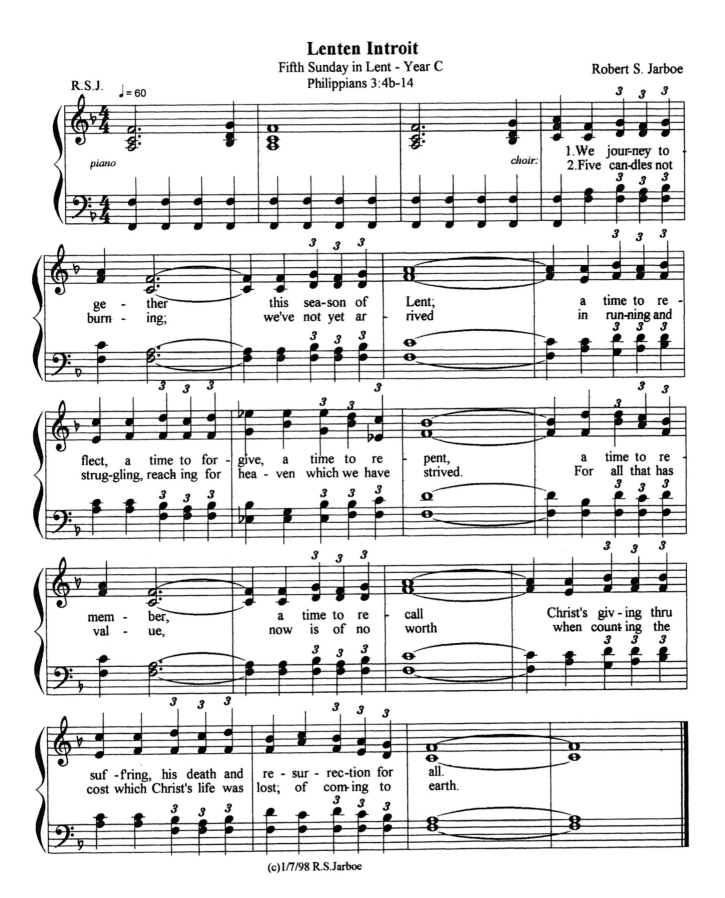

Year C — Passion/Palm Sunday

(Distribute this sheet to the readers.)

Date: _____

Reader A: _____ Reader B: _____

Choral Introit
(While the first verse of the choral introit is being sung, Readers A and B come forward and stand beside the Lenten candles. Reader B should bring a Bible.)

Litany
From Psalm 118:19, 20, 27

Reader A: Please turn to the Lenten litany in your bulletins:
(Pause until the congregation is ready)
Let us enter God's gates of justice with thankful hearts.
Anyone who is right with God can enter.
This is God's day to celebrate.
Palm branches at the altar mark our celebration.

Scripture
Reader B: Our scripture for this Passion/Palm Sunday is taken from Paul's letter to the Philippians, chapter two, verses five through eleven.
(Then read Philippians 2:5-11)

Extinguishing Of The Sixth Lenten Candle
Reader A: As we extinguish the sixth Lenten candle, we recall that God's Son, Jesus Christ, became like one of us so that we may have access to God and this became possible through Christ's death on the cross.
(While Reader A is speaking, Reader B takes the candle snuffer and extinguishes the third candle on the right.)

Prayer
Reader B: Let us pray: *(pause)* O God, what Christ has done for you and for us is truly wondrous. Even though he was your Son, he humbled himself for us on the cross. We truly agree, "Jesus Christ is Lord!" Amen.

Choral Introit
(While the second verse of the choral introit is being sung, the readers may be seated.)

Note: Should one of the readers be unable to read, let one do the reading while the other extinguishes the light.

Lenten Introit

Palm/Passion Sunday - Year C
Philippians 2:5-11

Robert S. Jarboe

Year C — Good Friday
(Or the last half of Passion/Palm Sunday service)
(Distribute this sheet to the readers.)

Date: _____

Reader A: _____   Reader B: _____

Choral Introit
(While the first verse of the choral introit is being sung, Readers A and B come forward and stand beside the Lenten candles. Reader B should bring a Bible.)

Litany   From Psalm 22:1, 28
Reader A: Please turn to the Lenten litany in your bulletins:
             (Pause until the congregation is ready)
             My God, my God, why have you forsaken me?
             We hear you, Christ.
             Why are you so far away?
             Who has really caused the distance?
             Won't you listen to my groans? Come to my rescue!
             You are in control, O God. You rule over all.

Scripture
Reader B: Our scripture for this Good Friday *(or: for the Passion of this service)* is taken from Paul's letter to the
             Hebrews, chapter ten, verses sixteen through 25.
             (Then read Hebrews 10:16-25)

Extinguishing Of The Christ Candle
Reader A: As we extinguish the final Lenten candle, the Christ Candle, may we be humbled by what God has done
             for us through his Son, Jesus Christ. Until the great resurrection, we will be in darkness because of his
             death. But be in hope, for Christ's final victory will be soon.
(While Reader A is speaking, Reader B takes the candle snuffer and extinguishes the final candle that is lit.)

Prayer
Reader B: Let us pray: *(pause)* O God, this darkness is caused by what we have done and the only way that the true
             light can be returned is through your Son, Jesus Christ. Help our spirits retain the hope that Christ has
             overcome death — that Christ will conquer all — that our sins are forgiven — and that your Kingdom
             will truly be established. Amen.

Choral Introit
(While the second verse of the choral introit is being sung, the readers may be seated.)

Note: Should one of the readers be unable to read, let one do the reading while the other extinguishes the light.

Lenten Introit

Good Friday - Year C
Hebrews 10:16-25

Robert S. Jarboe

69

Year C — Easter Sunday

(Distribute this sheet to the readers.)

Date: _____

Reader A: _____   Reader B: _____

Choral Introit
(While the first verse of the choral introit is being sung, Readers A and B come forward and stand beside the Lenten candles. Reader B should bring a Bible.)

Litany   From Psalm 16:7-10
Reader A: Please turn to the litany in your bulletins:
(Pause until the congregation is ready)
Praise God, for he has guided us through the night.
God is always with us — as close as by our side.
Let us rejoice and be glad! Even our physical bodies have hope.
For God will not leave us in death — just as he has not left his Son in the tomb.

Scripture
Reader B: Our scripture for this Easter Sunday is taken from Paul's first letter to the Corinthians, chapter fifteen, verses nineteen through 26.
(Then read 2 Corinthians 15:19-26)

Lighting Of The Christ Candle
Reader A: This morning we light the Christ Candle to remind us that in Christ is life and that life is the light for all people. The light has pierced the darkness and the darkness can never overtake the light — the one true Light which is found in Jesus Christ.
(While Reader A is speaking, Reader B takes the small candle and transfers the light from the altar candle to the Christ Candle.)

Prayer
Reader B: Let us pray: *(pause)* O God, we give you praise, honor, and glory for bringing us new life through your Son, Jesus Christ. We rejoice in knowing that we will rise from death like Christ and, in so doing, will live eternally with you. Amen.

Choral Introit
(While the second verse of the choral introit is being sung, the readers may be seated.)

Note: Should one of the readers be unable to read, let one do the reading while the other transfers the light.

Lenten Introit

Easter Sunday - Year C
1 Corinthians 15:19-26

Robert S. Jarboe

Additional Music

Extended Introit Arrangement

Accompaniment To The Extended Introit

Accompaniment To The Introit

Lenten Introit

(Extended Version)
Easter Sunday

Robert S. Jarboe

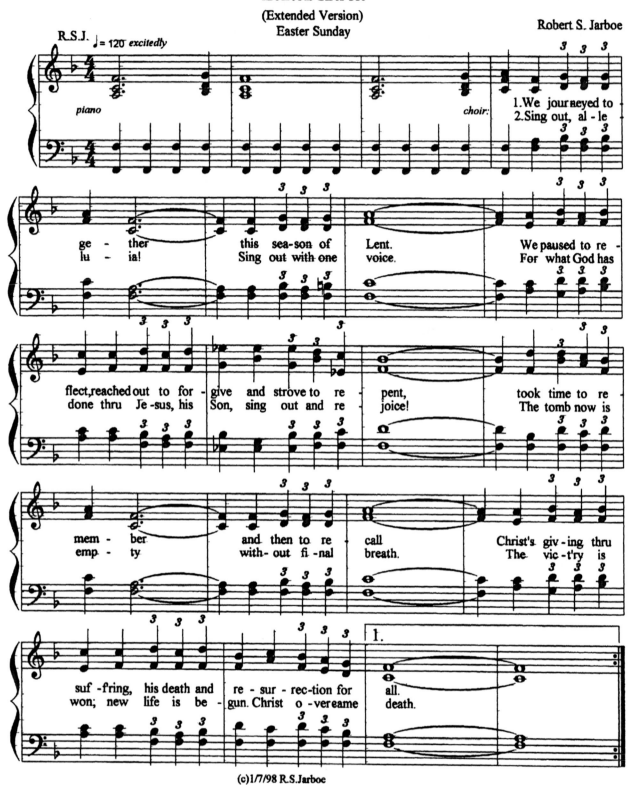

74

death. Sing al - le - lu - ia, sing al - le - lu

- ia. The vic - t'ry is won!

Lenten Introit
Extended Accompaniment
Easter Sunday

R.S.J. ♩ = 120

Robert S. Jarboe

piano

choir:

1. We jour neyed to ge - ther this sea-son of Lent. We paused to re - flect, reached out to for - give and strove to re - pent, to re - mem - ber and then to re - call suf - f'ring, his death and re - sur - rec-tion for all.

2. Sing out, al - le - lu - ia! Sing out with one voice. For what God has done thru Je - sus, his Son, sing out and re - joice! took time to re - emp - ty with- out fi - nal breath. won; new life is be - gun. Christ o - ver-came

The tomb now is Christ's giv-ing thru The vic-t'ry is

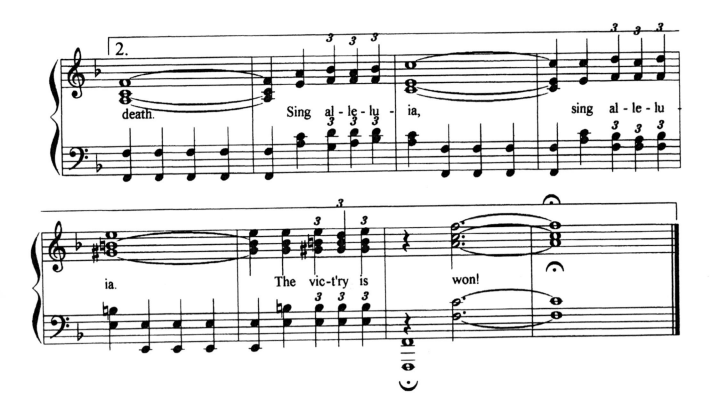

Lenten Introit
Accompaniment

CPSIA information can be obtained
at www.ICGtesting.com
Printed in the USA
LVOW09s1423210217
524948LV00025B/458/P